PANDORA

AN ARCHAEOLOGICAL PERSPECTIVE

Peter Gesner

Queensland Museum

Requests for this book should be made to:
Queensland Museum, Box 3300
SOUTH BRISBANE, Q 4101 Australia

National Library of Australia

Cataloguing-in-Publication data.

Gesner, Peter, 1949–
Pandora: an archaeological perspective.

    ISBN 0 7242 4482 4

    1. Pandora (Ship). 2. Shipwrecks – Queensland – Great Barrier Reef. 3. Underwater archaeology – Queensland – Great Barrier Reef. I Queensland Museum. II. Title.

    910.45

First printed 1991; reprinted and updated 2000

Editor: Michelle Ryan

Designed and Produced: Allan Isaak 1991

Typeset in Palatino Roman 10/12pt.

Printed on White Sapphire Dull 150gsm by Prestige Litho, Brisbane

Cover Photograph: Divers preparing an earthenware jar for recovery.
(Queensland Museum, Brian Richards)

Contents

* Surgeon George Hamilton's words from his journal. (Thomson, 1915: 143.)

Illustrations

Every effort has been made to trace the source of material used in this book, however the author and publisher would be pleased to hear of any omissions. The following institutions have kindly loaned material: National Portrait Gallery, England; British Library; National Maritime Museum, England; Royal Navy, England; National Library of Australia; and the Mitchell Library, State Library of New South Wales (SLNSW).

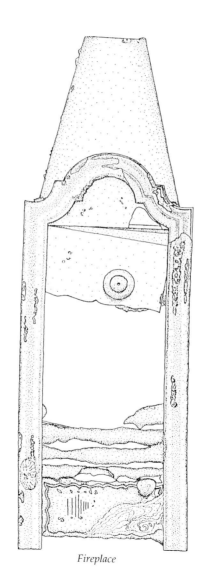

Fireplace

Stipple drawings throughout the book are the work of Bob Gerrard, Graeme Henderson, Bill Jeffery and Sally May.

Acknowledgements

Excavation of the *Pandora* has been supported and assisted by a wide variety of organisations and individuals. Direct financial support has been provided by: the Commonwealth Department of the Arts (DASETT), formerly the Department of Home Affairs & Environment; Castlemaine-Perkins Pty Ltd; Grace Bros Stores; the National Geographic Society; Flamingo Bay Research Charters; Frigate Rum; and the Inflatable Boat Centre.

Support in kind was generously donated by: Atlas-Copco; Comalco; David Flatman Productions; BP Australia Pty Ltd; Grace Bros Removals; NEC Information Systems; AutoDesk Inc.; Brian Kaye & Asssociates; Hanimex; Garner Agencies; Agfa-Gevaert Ltd; Engineering Testing & Research Services Pty Ltd; Sci Dive Australia Pty Ltd; Concut Pty Ltd; and Sportsuits Australia.

The Queensland Museum also gratefully acknowledges the support provided by several state museums and heritage agencies which seconded their staff to field work: the Western Australian Museum (WAM), the Department of Environment & Planning (South Australia); the Victoria Archaeological Survey (VAS); the Tasmania National Parks Service; and the Queen Victoria Museum (Launceston).

The author extends his special thanks to the volunteers from the Maritime Archaeological Association of Queensland who participated in field work, particularly: Robert McKinnon, Beryl Turner, Joe Sedlacek, Kevin McDougall, Fiona Scott, Colin Ward, Chapkin van Alphen, Maree Edmiston, Alan Mole, Don Norman, Anne-Marie Grice, David Bosisto, Jerry Calvert, Bob Gerrard and Paul Brown; and to volunteers Vickie Gillespie, Freya Bruce, Enid Waddington, Jan & David Vautin and Jessica Turner who have assisted the Museum's conservators with the treatment of *Pandora* artefacts.

Thanks are also due to the author's colleagues interstate for their professional assistance in the field: Graeme Henderson, Patrick Baker, Geoff Kimpton, Jon Carpenter, Brian Richards, Scott Sledge and Mike McCarthy (WAM); Bill Jeffery (Department of Environment & Planning, SA); Shirley Strachan and Peter Hervey (VAS); Paul Clark (Tasmania National Parks Service); and Mark Staniforth (Australian National Maritime Museum).

Also to colleagues — past and present — at the Queensland Museum: Sally May, Neville Agnew, Nic Clark, TC Good, Brook Batley, Mark McCafferty, Rosemary Eggleton, Derek Griffin, Michael Quinnell, Janet Campbell, Christine Ianna and Warren Delaney. To Ron Coleman for allowing me to consult the extensive notes he has collated during his research on the *Pandora* at various archives and libraries in the United Kingdom; to Allan Isaak for the design of this book; to Sally Elmer whose masterly eye for detail and perspective has resulted in several superb illustrations; and to Michelle Ryan for her editing expertise.

Facing page: An excavation team ascending from the *Pandora.* Divers can spend a maximum of only twenty-three minutes on the seabed and only two dives are allowed each day. *(Brian Richards)*

The Pandora

The *Pandora* was a 24-gun
Porcupine class frigate
designed by Sir John Williams.

Overall length : 114' 3" (35 m)

Length of keel : 94' 3" (29 m)

Breadth : 32' 2" (9.8 m)

Draught : 15' (4.5 m)

Tonnage : 513 tons

Armaments:

20 six-pound cannon,

4 eighteen-pound carronades,

12 half-pound swivel guns.

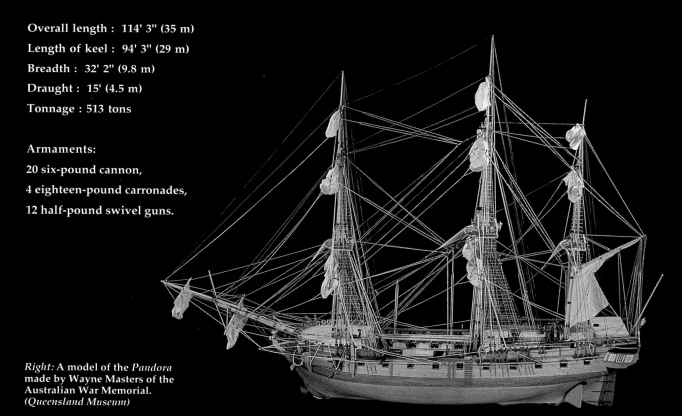

Right: A model of the *Pandora*
made by Wayne Masters of the
Australian War Memorial.
(*Queensland Museum*)

HMS Pandora: a chronology of important career events

February 1778

The British Admiralty contracts the Deptford shipbuilders Adams & Barnard to build the 24-gun frigate *Pandora*.

8 May 1779

The *Pandora* is launched at Deptford.

June 1779 – February 1780

The *Pandora* serves in the Channel Fleet under Sir Charles Hardy and Admiral Jervis; commanded by Captain Anthony Parrey.

May 1780 – December 1780

The *Pandora* serves as a convoy escort to North America (Quebec).

January 1781 – March 1781

The *Pandora* is refitted at Sheerness.

April 1781 – September 1783

The *Pandora* serves as a convoy escort to North America (St Lawrence River); commanded by Captain John Inglis.

October 1783 – June 1790

The *Pandora* is laid up "in ordinary" at Chatham.*

June 1790 – August 1790

The *Pandora* is prepared for active service with the Channel Fleet.

August 1790 – October 1790

Following special orders, the *Pandora* is prepared for service in "remote parts" (the South Seas). Captain Edward Edwards is appointed to command.

7 November 1790

The *Pandora* departs for Tahiti via Tenerife, Rio de Janeiro and Cape Horn.

2 February 1791

The *Pandora* rounds Cape Horn.

23 March 1791

The *Pandora* arrives at Matavai Bay, Tahiti.

11 April 1791

Fourteen *Bounty* mutineers imprisoned on board the *Pandora*.

May 1791 – August 1791

The *Pandora* visits the Cook, Union and Friendly Islands in search of HMS *Bounty*.

26 August 1791

The *Pandora* sights the Great Barrier Reef off the Murray Islands.

28 August 1791

The *Pandora* runs aground on a submerged reef in Pandora Entrance.

29 August 1791

The *Pandora* founders in 17 fathoms (30 m). Thirty-one *Pandora* crew and four *Bounty* prisoners drown.

16 November 1977

Divers locate the *Pandora* wreck site.

25 November 1977

The *Pandora* is declared an historic shipwreck under the Historic Shipwrecks Act (1976).

*If a vessel was described as "in ordinary" it meant she was temporarily taken out of service. An equivalent modern expression would be "mothballed".

A portrait of William Bligh, painted by John Smart, about ten years after the mutiny.
(National Portrait Gallery, England)

The Mutiny on the *Bounty* is probably one the best known sea stories from the annals of maritime history. This is largely due to four major Hollywood film productions which have all focused primarily on events at Tahiti, on the *Bounty* and at Pitcairn Island. The films have virtually ignored the exciting — and equally dramatic and tragic — story resulting from the British Admiralty's response to the mutiny which led HMS *Pandora* into the Pacific Ocean on what was to be her last voyage.

When Lieutenant William Bligh was cast adrift from the *Bounty* on 26 April 1789, his chances of reaching civilisation and reporting the seizure of his ship by master's mate Fletcher Christian were not good.

He faced several formidable obstacles. To begin with, the nearest European outpost was thousands of nautical miles away — the major part of the voyage being across ocean waters. And, to make matters worse, Bligh had been cast off in the *Bounty's* open 23-foot launch.

With eighteen men sharing Bligh's fate there was hardly any room for water and provisions — not that the mutineers had provided them with much in the way of stores, nor with many useful items such as firearms, maps and navigation equipment!

Presumably the mutineers had acted with some forethought, anticipating that with few weapons and stores the castaways would not be likely to survive. They knew that to properly equip the launch would only increase Bligh's chances of survival. In turn this would spell disaster for the mutineers who, of course, had a vested interest in ensuring that their actions on board the *Bounty* never became known.

Although it is not known what the nineteen castaways thought of their predicament, it is reasonable to assume they were all at least aware of the enormous odds stacked against them. Whatever their apprehension at the beginning of their open boat voyage, the castaways became acutely aware of their perilous situation after several days in the launch when they landed on Tofua. While searching for food and water, they were attacked by islanders and the *Bounty's* quartermaster John Norton was killed.

Norton's was the only death among the *Bounty* loyalists. The others suffered hunger, thirst and exposure during their 2200 nautical mile (3900 km) ocean crossing from Tofua to Great Barrier Reef waters.

Remarkably, they survived this ordeal and, after almost three weeks at sea, finally landed on an island off Cape Weymouth where they spent several days recovering from their deprivations. Bligh called their landing place Restoration Island — one of several features he named along the coast of Cape York Peninsula.*

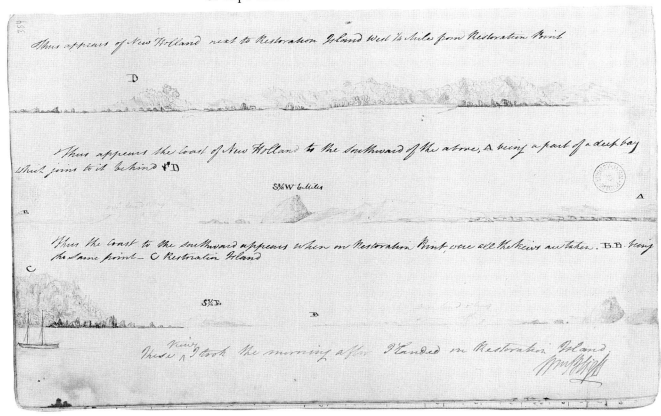

Views of New Holland from Restoration Island — a page from William Bligh's private log which he kept during his 5200 km ocean voyage in the *Bounty's* launch. A sketch of the launch can be seen in the bottom left corner.
(SLNSW, No 27)

* Some of these names are still used today — Bligh Boat Passage, Cape Direction, Sunday Island, Pudding Pan Hill and Booby Island. As for Restoration Island, Bligh could just as well have named it Bountiful Island, for the island's oysters and wild fruits were plentiful and helped restore the castaways' strength and spirits.

After six days in the relative calm of Great Barrier Reef and Torres Straits waters, the launch once again struck the open sea. This time the castaways had to brave the unpredictable Arafura Sea and their sufferings were as bad as any they had endured before. Battered by heavy seas and drenched by heavy rains, their progress was slow and what little strength they had regained was soon dissipated by constant bailing to keep the launch from foundering.

Living off odd catches of fish and birds, the castaways finally sighted the Timor coast and after several more days at sea reached the safety of the Dutch East India Company (VOC) settlement at Coupang. Their open boat journey had taken forty-one days and had covered 3600 miles (5200 km).

At Coupang they were received with considerable hospitality and after due attention to diet, health and hygiene they gradually regained their strength. Ten days after his arrival, Bligh had recovered sufficiently to negotiate the purchase of a small schooner which, with a length of 34 feet (10 m), was only slightly larger than the *Bounty*'s launch. The *Bounty*'s carpenter, bosun and sailmaker soon went to work to make the schooner ready for the next part of Bligh's homeward voyage.

Bligh and the loyalists being welcomed in Timor by the Dutch governor in June 1789.
(Charles Benezach, SLNSW, No 32)

Leaving Timor on 20 August 1789, Bligh reached Batavia in time to gain a berth in one of the ships returning to Europe in the VOC's October Fleet. After an uneventful voyage in the packet *Vlijt*, Bligh finally arrived in England on 13 March 1790 — almost one year after the mutiny. Having had ample time to prepare during his voyage from Batavia, Bligh was immediately able to provide the Admiralty in London with a full report.

The Admiralty, predictably, took a dim view of the mutiny and decided to send a warship to the South Pacific to recapture the *Bounty* and bring the mutineers to justice. They chose a 24-gun ship — one of a number of vessels then under-going a refit at Chatham in anticipation of hostilities against Revolutionary France. On 10 August 1790 the Secretary of the Admiralty sent a note to the recently appointed commander of HMS *Pandora*, Captain Edward Edwards, directing him to London to receive special orders.

1

In pursuit of HMS Bounty

Matavai Bay, Tahiti, sketched by
artist Sydney Parkinson during
James Cook's first voyage in 1770.
(British Library)

*". . . whereas the ship you command has been fitted out for the express purpose of proceeding to the South Seas in order to . . . recover the Armed Vessel [Bounty] and to bring in confinement to England Fletcher Christian and his associates . . . you are hereby required and directed to put to sea and proceed as expeditiously as possible to the Southward and shape your course around Cape Horn [and] steer for Matavai Bay . . . on the Northside of Otaheite . . ." ***

 Having received these orders from the Admiralty, Captain Edwards' objectives were clear. His mission was a policeman's: to find and capture the *Bounty*, hunt down the mutineers, and bring them back to England for trial and punishment. This was no easy task for although the outer limits of the South Pacific were known, it was still an enormous expanse of ocean with hundreds of uncharted islands where the mutineers could be hiding. Even calling at and searching all the charted islands would take more than a year to complete.

The *Pandora* sailed from Portsmouth on 7 November 1790 with a complement of 132 men. Whatever Edwards and his crew thought privately about their chances of finding the *Bounty* has not been recorded. The various extant journals and documents about the voyage do not give any clues, although the *Pandora's* surgeon George Hamilton mentions "alternate hopes and fears [taking] possession of [their] minds" as the English coast receded from view.

From the Admiralty's point of view, however, private "hopes and fears" were not of any consequence. What counted was their resolve to warn anyone in the Royal Navy who may have been entertaining similar "piratical" designs on one of His Majesty's ships. By sending the *Pandora* to the South Seas in pursuit of the *Bounty* mutineers the Admiralty's message was intended to be plain and simple: Do not pirate one of His Majesty's ships, for no matter how far away you are, no matter how safe or how strong you think you are, you will be sought out and brought to justice!

* Extract from Admiralty orders to Edwards (PRO/ADM 2/120 S BP 491).

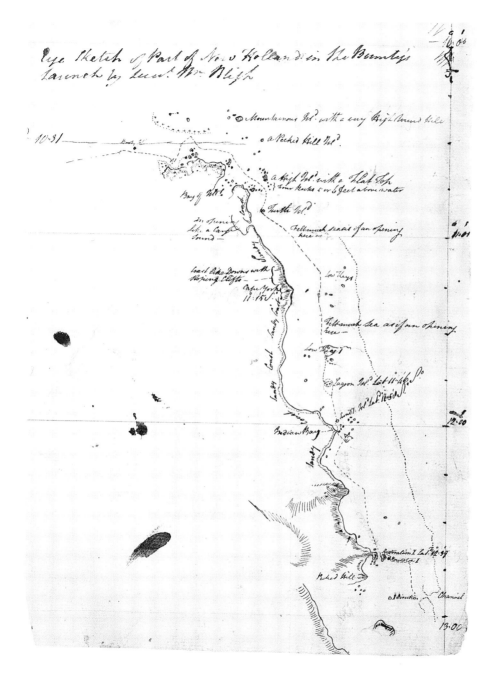

A chart by Bligh showing the route followed by the launch along the east coast of Australia. *(National Library)*

To give effect to this unequivocal message, the *Pandora* was loaded to the gunnels and provided with extra officers, midshipmen and able seamen as well as additional stores and fittings to man and refit the *Bounty*.

The *Pandora's* first port of call was Tenerife in the Canary Islands where a cargo of wine was taken on board for the crew. After a brief visit to Rio de Janeiro in early January 1791, the *Pandora* rounded Cape Horn on 2 February and set a direct course for Tahiti.

During this early stage of the voyage the *Pandora* came within one day's sail of Pitcairn Island which — unknown to Edwards — Fletcher Christian and his associates had found in January 1790 and where, soon after their arrival, they had set fire to and scuttled the *Bounty*. The mutineers were to remain undetected there until 1808.

Wine and beer bottles from the *Pandora. (Patrick Baker)*

The *Pandora* dropped anchor in Matavai Bay on 23 March 1791. The *Bounty's* armourer Joseph Coleman immediately came on board to surrender. His example was followed a few hours later by two of the *Bounty's* midshipmen, Peter Heywood and George Stewart, a master's servant Richard Skinner and the *Bounty's* nearly-blind fiddler Michael Byrne.

Early the next day three more seamen, Thomas Ellison, Charles Norman and James Morrison, also surrendered. These three had spent their time on Tahiti building a schooner in which they had hoped to sail for America or the Dutch East Indies.*

Within twenty-four hours of the *Pandora's* arrival at Tahiti, eight mutineers had given themselves up. From the information they gave about events after the mutiny, Edwards was able to ascertain that the *Bounty* had sailed off for an unknown destination in September 1789. Sixteen of *Bounty's* crew had elected to stay behind on Tahiti while eight of their former shipmates had chosen to throw in their lot with Fletcher Christian.

Of the sixteen mutineers on Tahiti, Charles Churchill and Matthew Thompson had been killed in a feud. With these two and the eight who had surrendered, ten of the twenty-five mutineers were accounted for. Edwards immediately made arrangements for the capture of the remaining six known to be hiding on the island. Armed shore parties were sent out to hunt them down and in a matter of days Henry Hildebrandt, Thomas McIntosh, Norman Birkett, Jonathan Millward, Jonathan Sumner and William Muspratt were also sharing the same fate as their former shipmates.

* By coincidence, the day before the *Pandora* arrived in Matavai Bay, the men had returned to Tahiti after setting out for Batavia. They had decided to abort their escape voyage because of problems with the schooner's sails.

They were manacled and locked away in a makeshift prison — referred to as "Pandora's Box" — which Captain Edwards had ordered built on the ship's quarter deck. As the prison was only 3.3 m by 5.4 m on deck and about 1.5 m high, the mutineers' existence was cramped and miserable. Armed sentries were placed around the prison and — presumably for fear some of the crew could be incited to mutiny or help with an escape attempt — the *Pandora's* men were ordered not to communicate with the prisoners.

Although he does not mention it in his account of the voyage, Edwards must have been feeling satisfied with his progress so far. However, he did not have any reason to be complacent as the eight mutineers who had joined Fletcher Christian and pirated the *Bounty* were still at large.

As for the whereabouts of the *Bounty*, Edwards did not gather any additional details which called for a change of plan or would have induced him not to act on his orders, which specifically listed the islands he was to search after Tahiti.

The *Pandora* remained in Matavai Bay for several more weeks, during which time her crew took on fresh water and provisions and prepared the captured schooner for duty as a tender.

On 8 May 1791 the *Pandora* sailed for Huahine — one of the Northern Society Islands — on the first leg of what was to be a futile search lasting more than three months and visiting most of the major Polynesian island groups west of Tahiti.

By August Edwards had begun to run short on supplies and had lost twelve men and two boats which had become separated from the *Pandora* during storms.* Edwards decided that further efforts to find the *Bounty* would be to no avail. On 15 August 1791 the *Pandora* set a westerly course for Timor via Torres Straits.

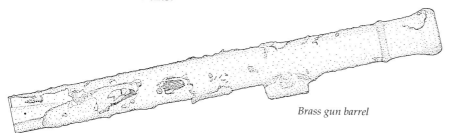

Brass gun barrel

* One of the lost boats was the schooner built by the mutineers. Command of the schooner had been entrusted to a master's mate William Oliver who, with a crew of seven, successfully navigated the schooner from the Samoan Islands, via the Torres Straits, to Sourabaya in the Dutch East Indies. The schooner had lost contact with the *Pandora* during a storm after the crew had gone ashore at Samoa searching for signs of the *Bounty*. This voyage under Oliver's command should be ranked with Bligh's much vaunted open boat voyage to Timor as an equally remarkable feat of navigation. A transcript of a journal of this voyage — kept by midshipman David Renouard — has survived and is of major historical interest, particularly because it describes Pacific islands not previously recorded by 18th century European explorers. The crew of the schooner arrived at Sourabaya before the *Pandora* survivors and, ironically, were imprisoned because the authorities had mistaken them for the *Bounty* mutineers. They spent several weeks in prison until Edwards arrived and was able to vouch for their identity.

2

An "exceeding dark, stormy night"

Pandora's masts protruding from the sea's surface — after a water-colour by midshipman George Reynolds. The boat which returned to the wreck salvaged some useful material from the masts and rescued the ship's cat. (*Allan Isaak*)

The *Pandora* reached the Great Barrier Reef on 26 August 1791 in the latitude of the Murray Islands and then skirted the outer fringe of the reef southward in an attempt to find a safe passage through these treacherous and uncharted waters.

Early in the morning of 28 August a promising opening was discovered and a boat was launched to reconnoitre. The boat, commanded by Lieutenant John Corner, set off in a south-westerly direction and was sighted again late in the afternoon. Corner had hoisted a pennant signalling that the opening was safe to navigate. As it was almost dusk, Edwards considered a passage through too dangerous and decided to wait until the next morning. Orders were given to pick up Corner's boat and stand out to ocean waters for the night.

This chart is based on one drawn by Lieutenant Thomas Hayward showing the *Pandora's* path as she searched for an opening in the Barrier Reef. *(Hydrographic Department, Royal Navy, England)*

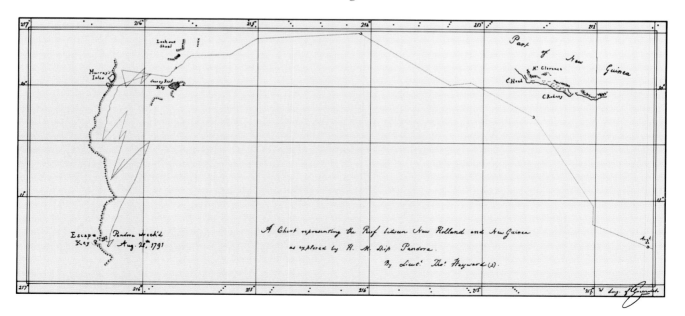

While manoeuvring to pick up the boat, the *Pandora* struck an isolated outcrop of submerged reefs nearly 4.6 km to the north-west of a sand cay at the southern end of the opening.

Unfortunately she had run aground sometime close to low tide and within an hour of striking the reef it was apparent that *Pandora* would not be refloated easily. With each wave she was driven further onto the reef, her bottom grinding heavily on the hard coral. The ship lost part of her rudder and steering gear and very soon afterwards, the carpenters reported that there was almost 8 feet (2 m) of water in the hold.

The frantic efforts of the men at the pumps produced results and after several hours aground the *Pandora* beat over the reef, aided by the rising tide. At about ten o'clock that night she was brought to anchor in relatively sheltered waters in the lee of the reef. Here, still buffeted by strong winds which had increased in strength since the afternoon, the crew spent an anxious night working desperately to save their ship.

An aerial view from the north-west of the reef area where the *Pandora* sank in 1791. West Reef is in the lower right corner of the photograph; Pandora Reef is in the upper left section; and Moulter Cay is in the distant background. The South Pinnacle is slightly to the right of the centre. (*Queensland Museum*)

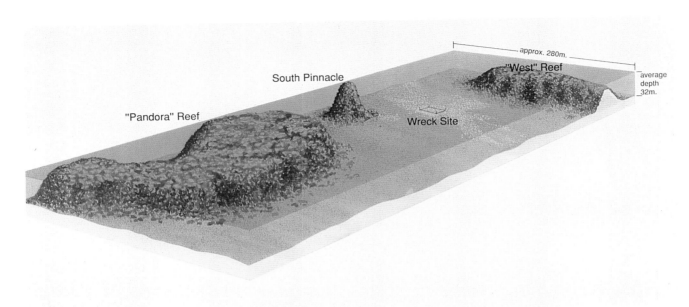

Above: An artist's isometric impression of the *Pandora* wreck site seen from the north-east. *(Sally Elmer)*

Right: Pandora Entrance and the wreck site. The area covered by *Pandora's* boat as she searched for an opening in the in the reef, is also shown.

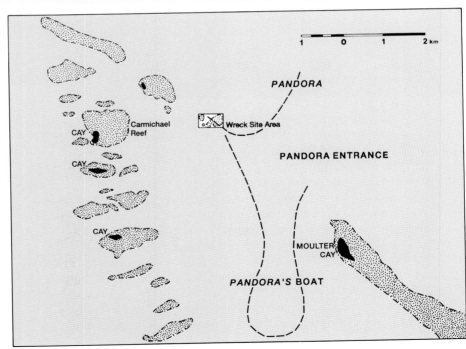

While the carpenters were below decks trying to repair the damaged hull, the rest of the crew were busy throwing the *Pandora's* heavy iron guns overboard to lighten the ship. For a moment it seemed that they might save the vessel, but disaster struck again. This time one of the pumps broke down and very soon afterwards the water level in the hold started to rise again. A last desperate attempt was made to save the ship by passing a sail under the damaged hull to stop the holes and stem the leaking.

All these efforts were fruitless and at first light on the 29 August Edwards and his officers agreed that nothing more could be done to save the ship. As the boats had already been hoisted out, they were provisioned in readiness for the crew's escape. Orders were given to cut loose from the decks any material which would float so that the men who could not swim would have something to cling to while waiting to be rescued by the boats. Almost immediately after these orders, the *Pandora* heeled over and sank within minutes.

The crew abandoning the *Pandora* — engraving based on an original drawing by mutineer Peter Heywood .
(Robert Batty, SLNSW, No 49)

During the night three prisoners, Coleman, McIntosh and Norman, had been allowed to help at the pumps. The others had been kept in "Pandora's Box" under armed guard and certainly would have drowned but for the humanity of the bosun's mate William Moulter who unlocked the hatch as he scrambled onto the prison to jump overboard.

Although all the prisoners, except Hildebrandt, managed to struggle out of "Pandora's Box", not all of them succeeded in breaking their manacles. Hildebrandt, Sumner, Skinner and Stewart perished with thirty-one of the *Pandora's* crew.

The survivors — eighty-nine of the crew and ten prisoners — spent three days on one of the sand cays near the wreck. During this time the four boats were prepared for the arduous voyage to Timor where the survivors hoped to find passage on ships bound for Europe. Before leaving the cay, a boat was sent back to the wreck to see if anything could be salvaged, but returned with only a few useful items and, incredibly, with the ship's cat which had been found clinging to the masthead.

Right: "Escape Cay"— engraving based on an original drawing by Peter Heywood. The mutineers, having survived the ordeal in Pandora's Box, were denied shelter in the makeshift tents.

Below: Although archaeologists are uncertain of the exact location of "Escape Cay", this small sand cay in Pandora Entrance may be the site. Apart from nesting turtles and birds, the cay is desolate. *(Brian Richards)*

While on the sand cay and during the open boat voyage the prisoners suffered unbearably. Their clothing had been in poor repair when they had been taken prisoner and they were not allowed to take shelter under the makeshift tents which had been pitched on the cay. And so, almost naked — their skin softened by three months of confinement in their dark prison — they were forced to bury themselves in the sand for protection from the burning tropical sun.

At noon on 1 September, after Edwards had divided the survivors into groups and distributed the remaining food and water, the boats departed from Pandora Entrance on their 1100 nautical mile (2100 km) journey to Timor. For Lieutenant Thomas Hayward, having been one of the loyalists cast adrift from the *Bounty* with Bligh, this was to be his second open boat voyage through Barrier Reef waters.*

The survivors' progress through the Barrier Reef and the Torres Straits was comparatively uneventful. Within twenty-four hours of their departure from the wreck they made landfall on the coast near Cape York where they found fresh water. In another twenty-four hours they safely passed through the Torres Straits into the Arafura Sea, which they traversed in ten days. They sighted Timor on 13 September and reached the Dutch East India Company (VOC) settlement at Coupang three days later.

Their reception by the authorities at Coupang was cordial. The Governor did everything possible to ensure that they made a speedy recovery from their ordeal. The mutineers' hardships continued; they were not treated with the same solicitude and were confined to the settlement's prison. Their situation was of course better than during their squalid confinement in "Pandora's Box", but for most of them there was to be no real improvement in their miserable conditions until after their trial on board HMS *Duke* in England.

Before reaching home, however, the prisoners were to become acquainted with several more gaols: the VOC ships *Rembang* and *Vreedenberg* in which they were transported to Sourabaya, Batavia and Capetown; and HMS *Gorgon* which took them on to Portsmouth.

After a six-day trial in September 1792, Byrne, McIntosh, Coleman and Norman were acquitted. Heywood, Morrison, Burkitt, Millward, Ellison and Muspratt were found guilty and sentenced to be hanged for their part in the mutiny. However, only three of these sentences were carried out. On the recommendation of the court, Peter Heywood and James Morrison were pardoned and William Muspratt's case was discharged on a technicality. Burkitt, Millward and Ellison were hanged in October 1792.

Captain Edwards and his officers were not indicted for *Pandora's* loss. The court of enquiry found no fault with Edwards or his officers and stated that the loss had been unavoidable after the accidental grounding.

Peter Heywood. Portrait by John Simpson. Heywood, then a 17-year-old midshipman, was pardoned for his part in the *Bounty* mutiny. He continued his naval career and rose to the rank of captain. *(National Maritime Museum, England, No 52)*

* Hayward had been assigned to the *Pandora* as the Admiralty felt that he could help identify his former shipmates.

3

186 years of solitude

The remains of *Pandora's* sternpost showing sheathing plates and gudgeons. *(Patrick Baker)*

The *Pandora* is one of Australia's best preserved shipwreck sites. After several seasons of archaeological excavation, an exciting variety of artefacts has been collected and it is estimated that about one-third of the hull is preserved beneath the sand.

Archaeologists can expect to find, buried within and around the hull, a complete and extremely coherent collection of objects which will shed new light on our understanding of what life was like on board a British warship engaged on a long voyage to the Pacific during the 18th century.

However, while that may be regarded as the ultimate objective of archaeological research of the *Pandora*, any study of the site should begin with an examination of how the ship broke up after sinking in 1791.

This type of examination helps archaeologists understand what human intervention and which natural deterioration and disintegration processes may have been at work and how these determined the condition of the wreck and the artefacts when *Pandora* was discovered in 1977.

An unidentified part of the *Pandora* wreck, heavily encrusted by coral, makes an ideal home for a variety of marine fauna. *(Patrick Baker)*

Looking at the human influences first, it is probable that after the survivors left the wreck, it remained undisturbed for 186 years. There is not any documentary evidence of salvage in the years immediately after *Pandora's* loss, though human disturbance before rediscovery cannot be ruled out.

Pandora Entrance is in an extremely remote area of the Barrier Reef far from regular shipping routes. During the late 18th and early 19th centuries, the closest Barrier Reef entrance used by European ships was at least 60 nautical miles (110 km) away to the north. So, if the wreck was visited at all, it is most likely that the visitors were Torres Straits Islanders.

Islanders on fishing or trading voyages could have sighted the trail of wreckage and flotsam and followed it to its source. They may even have collected material left behind on the sand cay by the survivors, but it is unlikely that they actually saw the wreck. It is possible that some may have seen the *Pandora's* masts protruding through the water's surface, but this clearly visible clue probably disappeared no more than a month or two after the wrecking.

Knowledge of the wreck's exact location within Pandora Entrance was most likely known only to the survivors and consequently, with the passage of time, this information was lost.

During the 19th century European shipping increased along this part of the coast — especially after the establishment of the Raine Island beacon in 1844. The closest major shipping route came within 15 nautical miles (27.7 km) of Pandora Entrance but there was still little reason for mariners to use this opening.

However, it is not inconceivable that pearling or bêche-de-mer skippers in the late 19th and early 20th centuries were vaguely aware that the *Pandora* had been wrecked somewhere nearby. It is possible that pearl divers searching the seabed for oysters could have happened upon the wreck, but we may never know whether they salvaged items from the seabed or disturbed the *Pandora* in any way.

The natural processes which had the most direct influence on the wreck were physical forces such as tidal currents and wave action, and biological ones such as marine borers.

The wreck is located well within Pandora Entrance; an opening about 5.6 km width on the outer fringe of the line of reefs which separates the Coral Sea from Torres Straits. The waters in Pandora Entrance therefore are not only exposed to the full force of ocean swells but are also affected by the strong tidal streams between the Coral Sea and Torres Straits. Consequently, fast flowing currents and rips occur across the site as large volumes of water are forced into and out of Pandora Entrance.

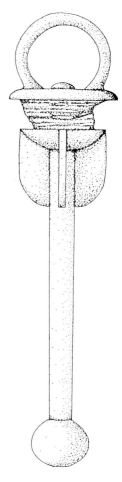

*Valve for hand pump
pulley system*

Possible stages of disintegration. *(Sally Elmer)*

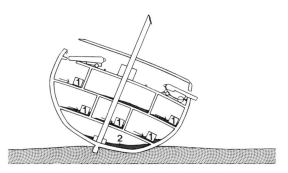

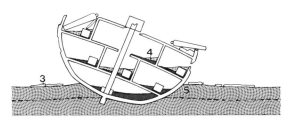

Stage 1 (Approx. one year after sinking)

Masts and rigging have broken off and floated away; weakened quarter and focsle deck bulwarks have broken off and been dispersed by currents. Small artefacts accumulate in clusters against internal partitions and bulkheads (1). Gradual silting-up begins as organic materials decay and fine particles are trapped within enclosed hull spaces (2).

Stage 2 (Approx. one to ten years after sinking)

Parts of the upper deck deteriorate and collapse due to marine borer activity. Some of the upper deck structural timbers fall away onto the seabed (3). Currents deposit coarser sediments into semi-enclosed hull spaces (4) and carry away and disperse light artefacts. Gradual seabed build-up occurs under and around the hull (5). Fine particle build-up continues within enclosed spaces.

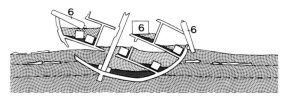

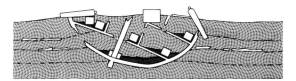

Stage 3 (Approx. ten to fifty years after sinking)

Continuation of processes started in Stage 2; more collapse of structural timbers; continued fine particle build-up in enclosed spaces and coarse sediment accumulation in semi-enclosed spaces. Seabed build-up continues around the hull. Heavy iron objects — eg cannon and ship's stove — drop down into lower areas of the hull (6).

Stage 4 (Approx. fifty to eighty years after sinking)

Wreckage approaches stabilisation. All spaces within the hull filled with compacted fine or coarse sediments. Seabed build-up has been completed. Marine borer activity ceases due to effective cover by sediments which insulate organic materials from oxygen.

Wave action certainly played a significant role in the *Pandora's* disintegration — particularly during the first few months after her loss, when it would have taken its toll on the wreck's protruding masts and rigging. As these were broken off, probably taking other parts of the superstructure with them, they were carried away by tidal currents.

After the hull settled onto the seabed it began to deteriorate almost immediately. Marine borers ate away at all the structural timbers and lighter woodwork. As a result, supporting beams lost their strength and caused decks, bulkheads and bulwarks to collapse.

When this happened more of the vessel's interior became exposed to the elements. Now, currents again came into play, either because they carried away lighter objects stowed within the vessel, or because they deposited sand into spaces and compartments inside the hull.

At this stage of the disintegration process, the direction and strength of current flow over the wreck was a particularly important factor because it also determined how rapidly sediment build-up around the hull occurred, how fast the hull settled into the seabed and was covered up, and how far away from the wreck objects from within the hull were dispersed.

Although these environmental influences all contributed to the partial deterioration and disintegration of the *Pandora*, paradoxically, they also contributed to her preservation.

The *Pandora* is not what is referred to as a "typical" Barrier Reef wreck. It is not like the site of a wrecked wooden or iron vessel which remained aground on a reef to be rapidly pounded to pieces by waves and scattered over a large area by the combined effects of winds, currents and waves.

What distinguishes Pandora from most other reef wrecks is that, after running aground, she did not remain stuck fast on the coral rocks. Pandora was refloated by her crew and brought to anchor in relatively deep waters where she subsequently sank and, still virtually intact, settled into a soft, sandy seabed.

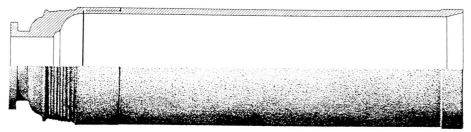

Bilge pump cylinder

4

Rediscovering the Pandora

Divers descending along the face of the South Pinnacle. At the base of the Pinnacle, archaeologists have found delicate artefacts light enough to be dispersed from the wreck by the currents.
(Brian Richards)

1977 Search: As the sequel to the infamous and much romanticised *Bounty* mutiny, the history of the *Pandora's* last voyage has an inherent ability to appeal to the imaginations of a large audience world-wide. So it is hardly surprising that, with the advent and popularity of scuba diving, various deliberate attempts were made to find the wreck.

During the late 1960s and early 1970s several haphazard searches were made in and around Pandora Entrance, but the wreck's position proved difficult to locate. It was obvious that more sophisticated search methods would be required.

In November 1977 the English documentary film-maker John Heyer teamed up with naturalist Steve Domm. They hoped to find the site with the assistance of an RAAF Neptune aircraft carrying out an airborne magnetometer search.

Sailing from Cairns in Steve Domm's yacht *Reverie*, they made for Pandora Entrance where, in anticipation of the Neptune's arrival, they marked out several search areas. Their choice was based on the results of archival research which Heyer had carried out in England where detailed documentary evidence about the circumstances of the *Pandora* wreck had been found. With this information it was possible to determine more exactly where the search should be concentrated.

Before the Neptune's arrival, the *Reverie's* crew met up with adventurer Ben Cropp in his vessel *Beva*. Eager to participate in this new discovery attempt, Cropp also delineated search areas for the Neptune and carried out visual searches along several larger reefs in the north of Pandora Entrance.

The Neptune had only a few hours to carry out a patterned search of the marked areas but after methodically covering all of them, none had produced any magnetic readings which might have indicated wreckage. With only a few minutes to spare before returning to base, the Neptune made a final pass over a small cluster of isolated coral outcrops on the edge of the main search area.

Here, the magnetometer registered a small disturbance in the magnetic field. Radioing *Reverie* and *Beva*, the pilot reported the find and dropped several smoke flares to mark the spot. *Beva* was the faster of the two vessels and the first to reach the flares before currents and waves caused them to drift away.

Placing several buoys to mark where the flares had fallen, *Beva* anchored close by and her divers immediately searched the seabed, certain they would soon return to the surface in triumph. But during this first dive they did not find anything.

Late in the afternoon, *Reverie's* divers also searched near the buoyed area, but they too found nothing. The two teams called off the search and made for their overnight anchorages behind Pandora Cay* to work out a plan for the next day.

Steve Domm and John Heyer decided on a methodical approach and chose to conduct another, more exact magnetometer search near the marker buoys. They opted to tow their detector behind *Reverie* in the area between two coral reefs to the north-west of the buoys, covering the seabed more thoroughly than had been possible with the Neptune.

Ben Cropp decided to take a chance and, making a reasoned guess as to where the wreck might be, planned to search the base of an elongated reef near the buoys. *Beva* dropped anchor in an area between the elongated reef, a small detached "bommie" and a moon-shaped reef[†] and Cropp asked one of his divers, Ron Bell, to search the seabed.

This turned out to be a good choice for, just as *Reverie's* magnetometer was approaching *Beva's* anchorage, Ron Bell surfaced, indicating he had found what so many divers before him had been looking for. By chance *Beva's* anchor had been dropped virtually into the middle of a flat sandy area which contained a large scatter of wreckage at a depth of just over 30 m.

The most prominent objects Ron Bell discovered on the seabed were a large Admiralty pattern anchor, a number of cannon, a large section of copper hull sheathing, an iron stove and several bronze rudder fittings. Digging into the sand, divers also found a number of bottles and a large ceramic jar (an "Ali Baba" jar).

One of *Pandora's* main anchors ("best bower"). Because anchors are usually stowed in the bow, archaeologists originally thought this anchor was in the forward part of the wreck. Subsequent analysis has shown that it is in the stern and is probably one of the anchors dropped underfoot to steady the ship immediately after *Pandora* was refloated from the reef.
(*Patrick Baker*)

*Now officially renamed Moulter Cay after bosun's mate William Moulter, in recognition of his humane action. (see pages 14 and 15.)
[†]Now referred to respectively as "West Reef", "South Pinnacle"and " Pandora Reef". (See diagram, page 14.)

While carrying out further searches around the wreck area, divers also located some rudder fittings on top of Pandora Reef. This indicated that the wreck which had been found on the seabed first struck the reef and lost some of its rudder gear before sinking.

Surely the wreck had to be the *Pandora*! After all, this agreed with the contemporary accounts which indicated that the *Pandora* had spent several hours aground before she beat over the reef. The *Reverie* and *Beva's* crews were certain they had finally located the *Pandora* and, in keeping with the requirements of the then recently proclaimed Historic Shipwrecks Act (1976), the discovery was reported to the Minister for Home Affairs and Environment in Canberra.

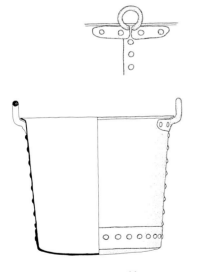

Large copper cauldron

The Historic Shipwrecks Act

The Historic Shipwrecks Act protects wrecks or shipwreck relics which are considered to be historically important. The Act's main objective is to provide for long term conservation of significant wrecks which represent aspects of maritime heritage.

Responsibility for decisions about historic shipwrecks has been delegated to various State Government institutions — in Queensland, Western Australia and the Northern Territory, to the Directors of the State Museums; in South Australia, New South Wales and Tasmania, to Departments of Environment, Planning and National Parks; and in Victoria to the Victoria Archaeological Survey. Each of these institutions employ a number of maritime archaeologists and specialists.

The processes associated with this kind of decision-making are referred to as cultural heritage management or cultural resource management. A decision whether a particular wreck is — or is not — of historic significance depends on specific questions: for instance, did the wreck play a part in the discovery, early exploration or early development of Australia, is the wreck associated with an event or person of historic importance or is the wreck a possible source of artefacts of cultural importance?

As far as John Heyer, Steve Domm and Ben Cropp's discovery at Pandora Entrance was concerned, these questions could easily be answered positively. On the assumption that their discovery was actually the *Pandora*, it was considered a wreck of historic significance because at least three out of seven criteria used to invoke the Act applied:

- *the site was associated with an event of historic significance (the Bounty mutiny),*
- *the site was a source of artefacts of cultural significance, and*
- *the site was an example of a particular maritime development (18th century European maritime exploration of the Pacific).*

Tentatively identified as the *Pandora*, the site was immediately protected under the Act. [1]

1 Commonwealth of Australia Gazette no. S 270 (25 November 1979).

Archaeologists surveying the wreck site in 1979. The Admiralty anchor's fluke can be seen in the foreground. *(Patrick Baker)*

1979 Archaeological assessment survey: To assist with decisions regarding the long term management of the site as a heritage resource, the Minister for Home Affairs and Environment commissioned an assessment survey of the wreck.

The objectives of this survey were:
- to confirm the wreck's identity,
- to assess its cultural significance, and
- to report on the possibility of retrieving artefacts for research and public display.

This survey was led by Graeme Henderson, a maritime archaeologist from the Western Australian Maritime Museum in Fremantle. In April 1979 he and his colleague, photographer Pat Baker, joined Steve Domm and Ben Cropp on board the Department of Transport's MV *Lumen* which had been diverted from her usual maintenance runs of navigation aids along the Queensland coast to take the survey team to the wreck.

The *Lumen* arrived at Pandora Entrance on the afternoon of 20 April 1979. Weather and sea were favourable for diving and the wreck was soon relocated and buoyed. Making the most of the good conditions, Henderson and Baker entered the water to inspect the site.

Two more dives were made the next day during which preliminary mapping and a close inspection of all visible features were carried out. As getting an overall view of the site was an important survey objective, Pat Baker took a series of photographs of the seabed for a photomosaic.

Unfortunately by 22 April the weather had deteriorated and prevented further diving so the *Lumen* left Pandora Entrance taking the archaeological team to Cairns.

The survey report by Graeme Henderson confirmed that all material evidence pointed to a wreck of a Royal Navy vessel dating from the late 18th century and consequently the site was positively identified as the *Pandora*. One of the most conclusive pieces of evidence was a rudder pintle which had been retrieved from the reef top. The markings on the pintle showed that it had been manufactured at the Forbes foundry, a known supplier of bronze ship's fittings to the Royal Navy in the 18th century.

Detail of the pintle found on Pandora Reef. The broad arrow and manufacturer's name embossed on the surface helped archaeologists identify the site as the *Pandora*. (Patrick Baker)

From the ordered distribution of the wreckage on the seabed, it was surmised that the vessel's hull had not been damaged by much physical disturbance once it had settled.

Although the vessel's quarter and focsle decks, as well as most of its upper deck, appeared to have disintegrated completely, Henderson suggested that much of the lower portion of the hull probably had survived as an intact structure buried in the sand. Because of this, the wreck was regarded as an extremely valuable archaeological and historic site. [2]

2 Henderson, 1986:131-134.

Using a classifying system proposed by the British maritime archaeologist Keith Muckelroy [3], the site was rated as a "first class" wreck which would prove to be one of the best preserved in Australian waters.*

Henderson suggested that the *Pandora's* stores, equipment and crew's possessions would most probably be found in superb condition within and around the remaining hull structure. Consequently a full archaeological excavation of the site was recommended.

In view of the wreck's tremendous potential, it was also recommended that a protected zone be declared around the site to prevent illicit or accidental disturbance. A "no entry" zone, covering an area within a radius of 500 m from the wreck, was proclaimed in June 1981.[4] This declaration is still in force and the protected zone may only be entered with a permit from the Minister or from the Minister's delegate — currently, the Federal Minister for the Arts, Tourism & Territories or the Director of the Queensland Museum.

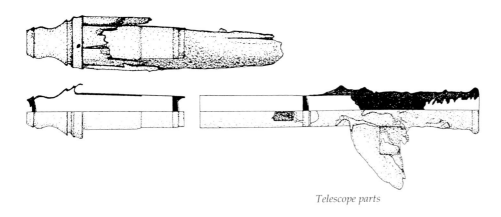

Telescope parts

*Keith Muckelroy's classification system rates wreck sites into five classes according to the extent of their survival. For example, a "first class" site has extensive structural remains and highly coherent artefact distributions, whereas a "fifth class" site has no structural remains and highly scattered or disordered artefact distributions. In a comparative study of twenty shipwreck sites, Muckelroy has demonstrated that environmental factors such as wave action and type of seabed influence the determination of a wreck's rating.

3 Muckelroy, 1978:162-65.
4 Commonwealth of Australia Gazette no. S 110 (5th June 1981).

5

Excavating the Pandora

Archaeologists recording the
position of artefacts within a grid.
This type of measuring takes up the
greater part of the divers' time on
the seabed. *(Patrick Baker)*

1983 First season: In October 1983 a first season of major archaeological excavation began. This was funded by the Commonwealth Government and organised by the Queensland Museum which, in 1981, had accepted responsibility for administration of the Historic Shipwrecks Act in waters off the Queensland coast.

Planning for the first season had started early in 1982 at the Museum's recently established Maritime Archaeology Section under the guidance of its Curator, Ron Coleman. In terms of personnel this expedition was a national effort, with participation of maritime archaeologists, conservators, and specialist technicians as well as volunteer divers from Western Australia, South Australia, Queensland, Victoria and Tasmania.

The excavation was directed by the Western Australian Museum's maritime archaeologist Graeme Henderson and its main purpose was to gather information about the site which would help determine how much of the hull was buried in the seabed.

A host of additional information about the site also would be sought for future planning: data on what problems divers would encounter while working at depths of between 30 m and 33 m, as well as the most effective methods for the safe recovery of artefacts.

Sailing from Cairns in the RV *Flamingo Bay* an archaeological team of twenty-two people arrived on site in late October. As a first priority survey marks were established to provide permanent reference points over a 20 m by 50 m area on the seabed around the visible wreck remains.

As this season's main objectives were to ascertain the orientation and exact extent of the buried hull and to collect a representative sample of ship's fittings, stores and crew's possessions, it was decided that small trenches should be dug in the aft, midships and bow areas.[5]

Using airlifts to remove the covering layers of sand, archaeologists started work in trench 1 which covered the sternpost. In this trench the intention was to dig around the sheathing and to follow the sternpost to its junction with the keel.

5 Henderson, 1986: 136.

Above: Divers establishing one of the permanent survey markers in the seabed, one of a dozen around the perimeter of the wreck. Up to 3 m of these 6 m poles is hammered into the sediment to ensure that they remain in place. The markers are used as reference points for all measuring on site. *(Patrick Baker)*

Left: Detail of the sternpost sheathing showing the draught marks in Roman numerals. In this photograph, the number XII indicates that an additional 12 feet (3.6 m) of sternpost remains under the sand. *(Patrick Baker)*

As excavation proceeded, draft marks were exposed indicating that at about the IX foot mark the sternpost had heeled over toward the starboard side of the hull. A large area of sheathing plates which had been attached to the port side of the hull was found. As these plates had crumpled onto one another, they formed a difficult barrier and prevented archaeologists continuing excavation in this area. After several more days of work it was decided that the junction of sternpost and keel could not be reached easily and trench 1 was abandoned due to time constraints.

Trench 2 was established in the bow area of the site. It was hoped excavation in this 2 m by 5 m grid would expose what was expected to be the bow of the remaining hull. Several large earthenware water storage jars — Ali Baba jars — and rigging and rudder fittings were uncovered and , beneath these artefacts, a large section of hull timbers was revealed in a good state of preservation.

In trench 3 — a probe of 2 m by 2 m in the midships area — a temporary grid frame was erected around one of *Pandora's* twenty-four cannon which had been selected for raising. Before this could occur, the surrounding sand had to be sifted and cleared away so that no small or fragile artefacts would be damaged or lost in the process of lifting the cannon to the surface. This precaution paid off because buried in the sand beneath the cannon was a gold and silver fob watch, almost unrecognisable because of its corroded condition.

A large collection of other delicate artefacts was uncovered in this trench. Many of these were medical implements and it has been suggested that this area corresponds to either the ship's surgery or the surgeon's cabin on the *Pandora's* lower deck.

button

With all but one of the major objectives achieved, the results of the 1983 season were encouraging. The work confirmed Graeme Henderson's first assessment of the wreck. The excavation had proved that, despite the deterioration of the vessel's quarter, focsle and upper decks, conditions at the site had provided a stable preservation environment for that part of the hull which had not deteriorated.

Although on-site conditions also presented some formidable operational problems for further full scale excavation, archaeologists were optimistic that these difficulties could be overcome. The large quantity and diverse range of artefacts, which had survived and which lay buried in the sand, ought therefore to be systematically retrieved for research and public display. Further, meticulous, archaeological excavation over a number of seasons was recommended.

The work so far indicated that the *Pandora* was a rich storehouse and that excavation would provide the largest collection of artefacts retrieved from a single 18th century shipwreck in Australian waters. By excavating the wreck using exact archaeological methods, it would be possible to use the retrieved artefacts to reconstruct in detail daily life on board.

Some of the medical equipment found under the cannon in 1983, left to right: a tourniquet clamp, a syringe (front), a marble mortar and a vial which contained traces of clove oil (presumably used as an analgesic). The syringe was used for the treatment of the "pox" (venereal disease).
(Queensland Museum)

Left: Among the material revealed in the trench dug in the bow during the 1983 season was an Ali Baba jar. *(Patrick Baker)*

Below left: A diver checking a spoil heap for small material which may have been inadvertently sucked up from the wreck during airlift operation. *(Brian Richards)*

Below right: One of the six-pounder cannon being prepared for raising. Strops were attached to the cannon before it was winched to the surface. The *Pandora* had twenty such cannon. *(Patrick Baker)*

1984 Second season: Excavation continued in November 1984 during a second major season again funded by the Federal Government and organised by the Queensland Museum. This time, excavation was carried out systematically using moveable aluminium grid frames which had been specially constructed to interlock with the survey marks established in 1983.

Starting in grids 1 and 2, archaeologists cautiously excavated across the site progressing to grid 12. The predominant type of artefacts found were ship's fastenings such as bolts and nails and fittings such as gunport hinges and glass window panes. Due to this distribution of artefacts, archaeologists then changed direction and continued excavating along the central axis of the site toward the main area of wreckage.

By the end of the season, archaeologists had reached grids 52 and 71 which appeared to be well within the confines of the hull remains. In grid 71 divers again sighted some of the ship's timbers. These were frames and inner hull planking from the *Pandora's* breadroom.

Archaeologists recording artefacts in grid 2 during the 1986. season. *(Brian Richards)*

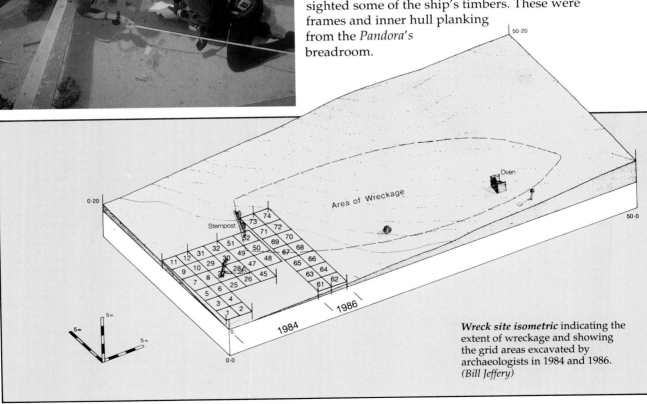

Wreck site isometric indicating the extent of wreckage and showing the grid areas excavated by archaeologists in 1984 and 1986. *(Bill Jeffery)*

One of the unique artefacts raised in 1984 was a compact fireplace which came from an officer's cabin — most probably the captain's or *Pandora's* great cabin — on the upper deck. By chance, the ash-tray belonging to this fireplace had been located near trench 1 in 1983.

As the exact orientation and extent of the hull had not been determined during the previous year, one of the 1984 season's objectives was to conduct a remote sensing survey with a sub-bottom profiler — a device which uses sound waves to probe the seabed. For this purpose, geologist David Johnson from James Cook University in Townsville spent several days on board the expedition vessel MV *Watersport* operating a sub-bottom profiler to record images of the buried hull remains.

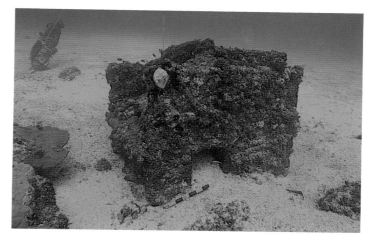

These images indicated that hull sections of about one metre depth in the aft area to around five metres in the bow have been preserved. Unfortunately, due to limited time, this could not be confirmed by excavation. However, work around the sternpost sheathing showed this interpretation of the profiler images was correct.

The images raised a number of questions about the hull remains. For instance, had decks collapsed or were they still in place? Did compartments and cabins still exist? Why did the images show hull sections of only one metre depth in the stern and up to five metres in the bow? The definitive answers to these questions would have to wait until another season.

Above: The iron Brodie stove from *Pandora's* galley — a prominent feature in the bow of the wreck standing about one metre proud of the seabed. The base of the stove is still buried in the sand.
(Brian Richards)

Left: The portable fireplace from the captain's cabin or great cabin on *Pandora's* upper deck. The fire box was made from copper sheet and lined with cast iron. It featured a wrought iron guard and heavily decorated brass surround.
(Brian Richards)

In the meantime archaeologists and conservators occupied themselves with the lengthy tasks involved in processing material retrieved from the site (for example, photographing, measuring and drawing each artefact).

A substantial number of artefacts required complicated conservation treatment. This was especially the case with the gold and silver fob watch and the iron cannon which had been recovered in 1983. Conservation work on most artefacts was carried out by Christine Ianna and Neville Agnew of the Queensland Museum. A few items were treated by the Western Australian Maritime Museum's conservators Ian McLeod and Jon Carpenter.

Right: Queensland Museum conservators applying tannic acid to the six-pound gun raised in 1983. After the coral growth had been chipped away from the surface, the gun was immersed in a caustic solution and underwent electrolysis to remove salts to prevent further corrosion. *(Queensland Museum)*

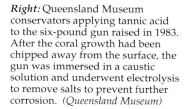

Above: Detail of the cannon showing the coat of arms of George III. *(Queensland Museum)*

1986 Third season: The third Queensland Museum expedition was joined by volunteers and the British-based youth, adventure training organisation "Operation Raleigh". This was the largest expedition mounted to the site, involving thirty-seven divers, seventeen ship's crew and twenty "Operation Raleigh" staff.*

In terms of diving operations, it was also the most complex expedition, due partly to the number of divers and partly to the size of the expedition's mother ship, the *Sir Walter Raleigh*.

*Previous expedition teams had not been larger than twenty-five.

Systematic excavation continued within the interlocking mobile grid network. Sixteen grid squares were erected between the aft and midships areas of the site, covering 64 sq m. As work progressed, dense concentrations of artefacts were uncovered. Like the artefacts encountered in trench 3 during 1983, these were mostly from within the hull remains and were in exceptionally good condition.

Six grids were especially rich in material and, most importantly, also contained more well preserved hull timbers. Analysis of the wood has suggested that the timbers correspond to the lower deck level where cabins occupied by the *Pandora's* officers were situated.

The artefacts retrieved from within the grids ranged from navigation instruments, sand-timers, crockery and wine glasses to a partially preserved flintlock pistol. An impressive collection of Pacific sea-shells and Polynesian tools and weapons was also found. These had most probably been acquired by one of the *Pandora's* officers with a view toward selling them to collectors of "artificial curiosities"* in England. Alternatively, it has been suggested that these Polynesian items may have been part of the belongings of either of the *Bounty* midshipmen Peter Heywood or George Stewart and were confiscated by Edwards when they were taken prisoner.

Below: Brass finial, probably a fireplace ornament. *(Queensland Museum)*

Above: Sand-timer bottles of various sizes recovered from the wreck. Sand-timers were used to determine the speed of the vessel. *(Queensland Museum)*

Left: A cluster of artefacts in grid 70. This distribution reveals how closely packed the artefacts are found. Archaeologists record the location of each artefact in three dimensions to the nearest centimetre. *(Brian Richards)*

* This term was commonly used in the 18th century to describe souvenirs collected by travellers in exotic places.

Above: A diver examining some of the ship's timbers sighted during the 1986 expedition. Oak was used exclusively for building naval ships and has withstood the ravages of two centuries under water. *(Brian Richards)*

Centre: A flintlock pistol. Treatment of this pistol is complicated because most of the wooden stock has probably deteriorated. However the encrustations have retained the original shape of the pistol so a replica can be cast. *(Queensland Museum)*

Far right: An encrusted storage jar. *(Queensland Museum)*

Below: Part of a telescope — eyepiece and tube — recovered in 1984. *(Patrick Baker)*

Below left: This Creamware ceramic plate in a Royal pattern is typical of many produced in potteries around England during the 18th century. Plates like this were primarily used by the Pandora's officers. Ordinary seamen ate from wooden plates. *(Queensland Museum)*

An unexpected find from this area was part of a human skeleton. This gave rise to speculation that the bones were the remains of one of the prisoners from "Pandora's Box". However, this is unlikely because the bones were found buried deep within the ship and "Pandora's Box" was located on the quarter deck. A more plausible explanation is that they are the remains of one of the two crew members known to have been killed several hours before the *Pandora* went down. According to George Hamilton's account, one sailor was killed by a falling spar and the other crushed by a gun carriage which had broken loose.[6] It is assumed that, in the interests of keeping up morale among the other crew members who were working desperately to save their ship, the two dead sailors were taken below to the surgeon's cabin or the ship's surgery.

Analysis of the bones has shown that they are the remains of a male about twenty-two years old and about 1.65 m tall.[*] Unfortunately further identification is not possible. All that can be stated about this individual is that his name is among the list of thirty-one crew members who perished when the *Pandora* sank. Maybe future archival research will turn up an official document or personal journal giving the names of the two sailors.

Although not the easiest season, 1986 was certainly the most productive.[†] Over almost five weeks divers retrieved 786 artefacts, compared to 256 in 1983 and 283 in 1984. In terms of conservation, such a large number of artefacts can pose problems if preliminary treatment does not begin as soon as these items have been raised. In this regard the Queensland Museum's conservators had built on experience gained by their colleagues interstate and were able to efficiently process most of the material. The treatment of some artefacts was started in the field, while others needed to be packed away until conservators could take care of them in a laboratory.

One of the Polynesian "curiosities", this stone food or poi pounder is known in Tahiti as a "penu". It is about 20 cm high. Poi, an important food staple, is a starchy pudding made by pounding breadfruit, taro or bananas and matured by fermentation. *(Queensland Museum)*

---

* This analysis was carried out by Geraldine Hodgson at the University of Queensland's Department of Anatomy.
† Nor was it the happiest season — the waters around Pandora Entrance claimed the life of yet another British seaman. Able Seaman Neil Carmichael, a member of the *Sir Walter Raleigh's* crew, was lost at sea in tragic circumstances during his watch on the night of 8 November 1986.

6 Hamilton in Thomson, 1915:143.

6

A hatchway to the past

Detail of a silver and gold fob watch showing the manufacturer's name and serial number on the casement — J.J. Jackson, a London watchmaker. *(Jon Carpenter)*

After three seasons of major excavation, sufficient information has been gathered to describe, with some measure of reliability, how much of the hull and how much of the *Pandora's* cargo and crew's personal possessions have survived.

It is now possible for archaeologists to assess in more detail the potential of the *Pandora* wreck as a research, display and educational resource. Archaeologists and museologists are better able to consider what insights into the past can be gained from study of the *Pandora* material and how these can best be interpreted and displayed.

The cargo: There have been few cargo items, except for the Ali Baba jars, among the objects uncovered and retrieved to date. The explanation for this is simple. Like most vessels, the *Pandora* carried the bulk of her cargo in her holds which are at platform deck level — excavation has not reached this far down into the wreck.

It is known from archival sources that the *Pandora* was carrying a complete set of extra fittings and stores in anticipation of the need to refit and resupply the *Bounty* after her capture. This will probably present some problems for archaeologists as it will not be easy to distinguish between items intended for the *Bounty* and those which the *Pandora* carried as part of her own spares.

The crew's personal possessions: Items belonging to the crew are numerous and have been located in superb condition, especially in areas within the confines of the hull remains.

In the main, the crew's possessions appear to be from compartments which were used by officers on the *Pandora's* lower deck. Excavation has exposed large clusters of personal effects which have been deposited against partitions and onto the lower deck. More significant from an archaeological perspective is the fact that these clusters are separated by preserved portions of cabin partitions.

With careful reconstruction of the location of these artefacts and correlation with information on the occupants of cabins from archival sources, archaeologists should, in many cases, be able to ascribe artefacts to individuals.

Small finials — Surgeon's instrument handles

This has already been done with the gold and silver fob watch. Because of its association with medical equipment, it is believed to have belonged to the *Pandora's* surgeon George Hamilton. However, archaeologists cannot be sure of this, as it also could have belonged to James Innes, the surgeon's mate.

This example clearly illustrates one of the reasons why archaeologists think is is important that the position of each artefact be recorded exactly before it is removed from the wreck. The precise association of objects can help with their individual identification and may reveal to whom they belonged. If, in the future, items engraved "JI" are found where the fob watch was located, it could be concluded that these — and the fob watch — belonged to James Innes rather than Hamilton.

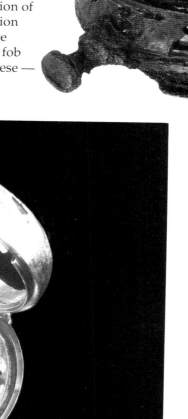

Above: The fob watch as it was found. *(Jon Carpenter)*

Left: Conservation treatment of the watch revealed a silver casing and gold filigree workings. With the addition of a few metal springs, the watch could be made to work. *(Jon Carpenter)*

Work on the *Pandora* site indicates that the focsle, quarter and upper decks have been lost. However excavation and sub-bottom profiler surveys suggest that the lower and platform decks, as shown on page 49, have been preserved beneath the sand. *(Sally Elmer, after John McKay)*

FOCSLE and QUARTER DECKS

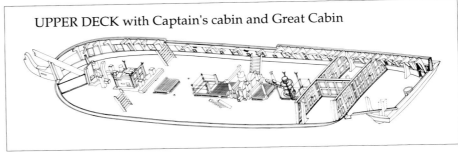

UPPER DECK with Captain's cabin and Great Cabin

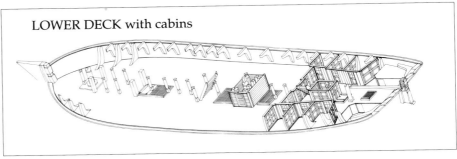

LOWER DECK with cabins

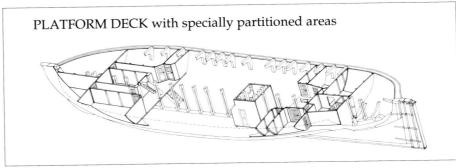

PLATFORM DECK with specially partitioned areas

The hull: From the 1986 excavation, it is evident that in the stern — aft of the *Pandora's* mizzen mast — the hull has almost completely disintegrated. The only intact timbers to survive from the aft area appear to be on the starboard side of the hull from approximately the level of the waterline (lower deck) down to the keel.

Using a photomosaic of the hull, together with 18th century Admiralty draughts of a 24-gun frigate and the sub-bottom profiler images, it is possible to suggest how much of the *Pandora's* hull may have survived in the seabed.

However some caution is called for. The artist's impression pictured below indicates that almost the entire lower hull, from lower deck level in the midships and bow sections, has survived. It also suggests that most compartments at platform deck level remain intact under the lower deck. This still needs to be confirmed by excavation.

It is also uncertain whether parts of the lower deck on the port side of the wreck have deteriorated completely or have collapsed into the hull. There is also doubt as to whether partitions on some of the platform decks have been preserved.

The only sure means of determining how much of the hull still remains will be to remove the sand layers covering the entire wreck. Perhaps this demanding and costly exercise will be undertaken at some time in the near future.

Artist's impression of the hull remains. Until *Pandora* is completely uncovered archaeologists will not be certain how much of the vessel still exists. *(Sally Elmer)*

Recent Developments*: Between 1996 and 2001, the Queensland Museum was able to embark on a new series of archaeological excavation comprising five major expeditions to the wreck and involving large teams of up to 40 individuals per expedition. Before this new series began, a small expedition was mounted in 1993 and a slightly larger one in 1995. These two early expeditions were quite different in character and purpose.

The objectives of the 1993 expedition were essentially management-oriented encompassing: gathering of sediment samples to assess the long-term biological stability of the wreck; experimentation with physical means of protecting the wreck site from environmental impacts; consecrating, and erecting on-site, a commemorative obelisk containing the skeletal remains of a *Pandora* crew member; and recording of more extensive remote-sensing images of the buried hull remains.

These objectives were formulated to determine how to effectively manage and protect the wreck in the long term. After all, by the late 1980s it had become clear that a program of on-going systematic excavation should no longer be considered feasible or desirable without a confident prospect of substantial on-going funding.

Above: Consecration by RAN Chaplain Mark Wallbank of the commemorative obelisk containing the skeletal remains of "Dick", 1993.

(Queensland Museum, Gary Cranitch)

* Since this book was first published in 1991, several remarkable developments have made possible the continuation of the archaeological work on the *Pandora* historic shipwreck and resulted in a major expansion of the Museum of Tropical Queensland. These developments were initiated in 1994 by Queensland's then Attorney-General and Minister for the Arts, the Hon. Dean Wells, who urged the Queensland Museum's Board of Trustees to establish the *Pandora* Foundation to conduct a fund-raising campaign and capitalise on a $1 million subsidy scheme offered by the Queensland Government. The *Pandora* Foundation was established in 1995. Comprising civic leaders and prominent members of the Greater Townsville business community, the Foundation subsequently launched a successful fund-raising campaign which, by mid-1996, had raised more than $2 million. With these funds, and the $1 million Queensland Government subsidy, the Museum's Maritime Archaeology and Conservation Sections were able to revitalise recovery and conservation work on the *Pandora*'s contents. In late 1997, after further lobbying by the *Pandora* Foundation on behalf of the Greater Townsville community, the Queensland Government announced that $18.3 million would be spent on a major re-development of the Museum of Tropical Queensland in Townsville. This expansion would accommodate the collection of artefacts recovered from the wreck and provide for a permanent exhibition telling the exciting story of the *Pandora*'s last voyage. Popularly referred to as the "*Pandora* Museum", the expanded Museum of Tropical Queensland opened in June 2000.

Consequently, by 1992 the decision had been made to discontinue excavation and concentrate on finding a long-term conservation strategy to protect the site from undue weathering, environmental influences and vandalism.

By the time of the 1995 expedition, however, it was possible to formulate an entirely different rationale as a result of the solid prospect of on-going funding. The 1995 expedition was conducted as a dress rehearsal for an anticipated series of five major expeditions, as well as to maintain the revitalised *Pandora* Project's momentum and continuity by providing publicity and promotional material for the *Pandora* Foundation's planned fund-raising campaign.

A 4-point mooring system was installed by a marine engineering contractor in December 1994 and was designed to hold the expedition's mother-vessel directly over the wreck. Having the mother-vessel in a secure position directly overhead was an absolute prerequisite for the deployment of divers using Surface Supplied Breathing (SSB) equipment.

Excavation work was conducted in two areas of the site between 20 January and 5 February 1995 by a team of 16 SSB divers, operating from the TSMV *Pacific Conquest*. Work underwater confirmed that the *Pandora* had settled onto its starboard side and that it was intact from the keel to approximately the waterline. However, it did not survive to the extent indicated by the artist's impression (see p.49). Substantially less of the portside structure appeared to be preserved and less of the lower deck was intact. On the other hand, the starboard structural remains were as substantial as indicated in the artist's impression (p. 49); but most importantly, the hull remains contain a well-preserved and coherent array of artefacts buried in the seabed in deposits of up to 3 m deep.

Since the 1996 season, excavations have concentrated in the stern and the bow. These were the areas of the ship used mainly for the crew's accommodation and for storage of their private possessions and professional equipment. Clusters of artefacts have been found here relating to the officers and the crew, shedding light on their various shipboard activities. During each season these clusters were recovered from areas of only 2 m by 3 m metres square and in deposits up to 1.5 m deep.

Above: TMSV *Pacific Conquest* on site with SSB divers in action. *(Queensland Museum, Gary Cranitch)*

1996 Expedition: Excavation was carried out in one area of the site only — in grid 89 (see below) — exposing part of the *Pandora*'s gun powder store (the magazine), as well as an area of the lower deck suspected to be the location of First Lieutenant John Larkan's cabin.

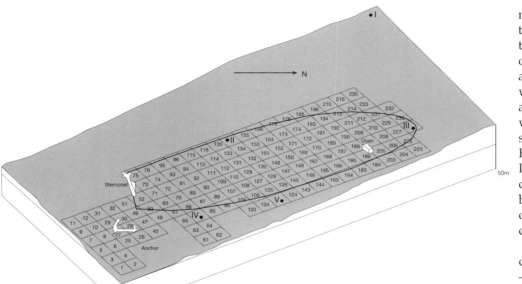

A diverse collection of material was retrieved from this cabin. The condition of the artefacts, especially the organic materials, was astounding. Of particular note was a cache of Polynesian artefacts, including seven wooden war clubs, carefully stowed for the voyage back to England. In addition to the Polynesian material, the collection included personal belongings, among them an octant, a name stamp and a chamber pot.

Adjacent to Larkan's cabin area, an intact partition — a bulkhead — was uncovered. It was found to extend under Larkan's cabin and was identified as the bulkhead separating the magazine from the captain's storeroom. Two intact tiers of powder kegs uncovered here confirmed that identification.

Human skeletal remains were also discovered in the cabin area. These were more complete than the remains recovered in 1986 (see p. 43) from the adjacent area and reinterred during the 1993 expedition.

1997 City of Townsville Expedition: Excavation was again concentrated in the stern section of the wreck site — in grids 88+90 and the adjacent grid 109 (see above) — and uncovered areas of the lower deck and the captain's storeroom on the platform deck. Approximately 70 per cent of the storeroom was excavated.

Lower deck area. A reference point established during the 1996 season served as a starting point for excavation of an area expected to contain the contents of the third lieutenant's cabin. However, after several days of excavation it was concluded that the cabin had actually been taken down at the beginning of the *Pandora*'s South Pacific voyage and the space used to store spare parts. This conclusion was inescapable because the anticipated

Above: Site plans showing grid locations excavated by archaeologists 1996–2000.
(Diagram Bill Jeffery)

concentration of personal belongings indicating a cabin area was not encountered.

Captain's storeroom area. The intact partition between the captain's storeroom and the magazine served as a starting point for excavation in this area. Using the partition as an excavation face, archaeologists almost immediately encountered a large collection of Captain Edwards' personal possessions, including a cream ware dinner set, tumblers and wine glasses. These were found on the forward side of the bulkhead, more or less arranged on the shelving as they had been stacked and stored by the captain's steward during the voyage.

Human skeletal remains were also retrieved from the storeroom area. Although the identity of the individual concerned has not yet been established, a cursory examination by Stuart Lavender, the expedition's medical doctor, suggested that he was a fairly stocky individual, perhaps about 1.65 m tall. These skeletal remains brought to three the number of individuals recovered from the wreck to date*.

In addition to temporary shelving, another partitioned area was located inside the storeroom. This low partition consisted of special casing containing at least two, possibly three, tiers of ceramic jars packed in sawdust.

Above: From Captain Edwards' dinner set: a cream ware soup tureen.
(Queensland Museum, Gary Cranitch)

* When the *Pandora* sank, 4 prisoners and 31 crew lost their lives. At the end of the 1999 season, the skeletal remains of three individuals had been recovered from the wreck. Because they have not yet been identified they have been nicknamed "Tom, Dick and Harry". In accordance with the British Admiralty's wishes, "Dick" was reinterred. This was done in a special service during the Queensland Museum's 1993 Expedition, when a consecrated obelisk was lowered onto the wreck site. The obelisk contained all of "Dick's" skeletal remains recovered in the 1986 season. A similar ceremony will one day be carried out for "Tom" and "Harry". However, before they are interred, it may be possible to identify the remains by matching DNA extracted from the bones with the DNA of living descendants (if they can be traced). DNA has already been extracted from "Harry's" bones by forensic osteologist Dayman Steptoe. "Tom and Dick" are possibly the two men fatally injured before the ship sank. They would have been taken below decks to be buried at sea after the crew had saved the ship. Their bones were found close together in the vicinity of the surgeon's cabin and first lieutenant's cabin. But what about "Harry"? Who was he? He was certainly drowned, but why were his bones found deep inside the wreck, inside the captain's storeroom? Did he have a reason for being in the storeroom? Was he one of the carpenter's crew, trying to repair the damaged hull? If so, he is possibly carpenter's mate Robert Brown. On the other hand, he may have been an opportunistic thief who was trapped below decks as the *Pandora* foundered. Alternatively, he was perhaps a scared and confused sailor who knew he wasn't going to survive so he was there to raid the captain's private wine stores, reasoning that to get roaring drunk one last time would be a good way to die!

Above: Facial reconstruction of "Harry" by Meija Sutisno at the New South Wales Institute of Forensic Medicine (courtesy of BBC Science).
(Queensland Museum, Gary Cranitch)

Having concentrated most of the excavation efforts in the stern during the 1996 and 1997 seasons, it was subsequently considered a matter of urgency to start excavating in the bow area of the wreck: the section where the ordinary seamen lived. This was undertaken during the two subsequent seasons: 1998 and 1999.

1998 Ergon Energy (NORQEB) and 1999 Port of Townsville Expeditions: *Bow section.* Excavation commenced in grid 181/83 and trended across the hull remains into grids 164 and 166 (see p. 52). The excavation was relatively shallow in grid 181 and along the baseline side of grid 183. However, it deepened as it extended into grid 185. As a result, the anticipated upper edge of the copper hull sheathing was encountered in grid 185, as well as the upper edge of the hull remains.

These timber remains are thought to be outer planking, parts of several frames and what appeared to be one of the lodging knees

supporting the lower deck. The exposed edge of copper hull sheathing and hull remains was followed aft for a distance of approximately 1.25 m until it was obscured by a mass of concreted material, including lead channelling (scuppering ?) and iron mast bands.

During 1998, the teams working the bow section were somewhat disappointed that no dense clusters of artefacts were exposed. This was attributed to not having penetrated far enough into the sediment. Before backfilling was carried out, some deeper exploratory probes were dredged adjacent to the Brodie stove in grid 185. This probing was continued in the 1999 season and resulted in the discovery of ethnological material — shell adzes, several fish lures and octopus lures, as well as shells ('natural curiosities') and coconut fragments. The probes also uncovered a semiprecious (intaglio) seal stamp, some sealing wax, a spirit bottle and a small medicine vial. Substantial parts of the ship's structure were exposed here as well; these timbers appear to be frames and outer planking.

Although the edge of the copper sheathing was encountered at approximately the expected location in grid 183, excavation has not yet been extensive enough to provide a definitive indication of the extent of hull remains in the bow, nor an exact indication of the precise whereabouts within the preserved hull remains. A number of timbers have been uncovered in a few small areas in the bow. However, identifying their original location (i.e. whether from lower deck levels or platform deck levels) has proved impossible, largely because they were obscured or obstructed by large, complex arrangements of concreted artefacts. After the 1999 season, it is assumed that excavation had reached somewhere in the vicinity of the carpenter's storeroom.

Stern section. During excavation work continued in 1998 and 1999, archaeologists penetrated deeper into the seabed (especially during the 1999 season) to a depth of up to 2 m. This work resulted in even more revealing clusters of artefacts being discovered. These were often found in their original storerooms and packing cases, as left behind in 1791.

From an archaeological perspective, these discoveries were particularly stimulating and revealing and provided insight into life on the *Pandora*, where space, even more than usual, was at a premium. For the *Pandora* was crammed to the gunnels with the stores required to provide for its own crew and ship's repairs, as well as a complete set of spares taken on board in anticipation of the need to repair and reprovision the *Bounty*.

Beyond 2000: Systematic excavation in the stern and bow sections is expected to continue in 2001 and should reveal more evidence to substantiate the suspected extent and structural integrity of the hull remains, especially of the lower starboard side. In this respect, exposure during 1999 season of the intact floor of the aft platform deck lobby is ample indication that the fish and spirit rooms are still intact and will be exactly as they were left more than 200 years ago. This is a priority area for excavation in the 2001 season. According to the existing architect's plans, the spirit room is located below the officers' store. Future excavation will investigate this space to confirm whether kegs of rum and bottles of gin were stored here.

The aims of the excavation series, started in 1996, are to recover the vessel's contents, in particular the objects that will reveal the social fabric of the crew. These objects make up the "real life" evidence of conditions on board a British warship in the South Pacific in the 18th century. The ability to pin-point the exact location of, among others, John Larkan's cabin may prove to be a key to understanding social structure and to shed some light on social fabric and life on board.

Above: Intaglio seal stamp recovered in the bow section during the 1999 dive season. Did its owner — probably an ordinary seaman — identify with Atlas, considering he bore the weight of the ship's heavy work on his shoulders?
(Queensland Museum, Gary Cranitch)

Who was John Larkan?

According to a brother officer, Surgeon George Hamilton, Larkan was
...a seasoned officer who was able to assert discipline amongst the crew in difficult and uncomfortable conditions.

According to *Bounty* mutineer James Morrison, he was an uncaring man, an officer with a somewhat sadistic streak in him. Not much more is known about him, at least not from archival sources. It appears that he came from Athlone in Ireland and his elder brother was a captain in charge of the Royal Navy Hospital in Greenwich; so perhaps it can be assumed he was from a naval family. Any other journals or letters he may have written, or records and diaries kept by brother officers mentioning him have apparently not survived.

Larkan's name stamp confirmed that the middle starboard cabin on the lower deck (see p. 48) was occupied by him. This cabin was barely large enough to move around in comfortably, being approximately 2 m by 2 m and 1.75 m high. Furniture probably consisted of a sleeping cot suspended from deck beams overhead, a writing desk and a stool. Most of his personal possessions would have been kept in his sea chest.

The artefacts found in the cabin provide us with interesting new information that possibly tells us more about the man. He could be considered a man of taste and refinement who kept his port in a decanter and used fine glassware.

The table at which he and his brother officers sat down to dine had all the trappings of any "middling class" table in Britain at the time, with brass candlesticks and fine Chinese porcelain tea bowls and saucers. According to Surgeon Hamilton, the *Pandora* was the first naval vessel to be supplied with tea, so Larkan may well have enjoyed the luxury of drinking tea on board.

Right: Larkan's name stamp, found among the objects in the artefact cluster provenanced to his cabin.
(Queensland Museum, Gary Cranitch)

Excavations have also revealed that Larkan may have been a collector of Polynesian artifacts, known as "artificial curiosities". The collection may been intended to remind him of the exotic peoples he had encountered during his Pacific voyage; or he may have thought of them as conversation pieces; but most likely he had hopes of selling them to collectors or museums upon his return to Britain.

Larkan's possessions mainly reflect private or personal aspects of his life on board the *Pandora*. The glass bottles may have been used to hold scented water. Perhaps the small bone or ivory handled brush — its bristles long gone — was it a wig brush?

Continued research involving comparisons with artefact assemblages from other wrecks of naval vessels of the period and future excavations may provide us with answers to these and other questions.

Above: Collection of Tongan war clubs uncovered in 1996 in John Larkan's cabin.
(Queensland Museum, Gary Cranitch)

Sources

Primary Sources:

Original copies of the Admiralty's Orders to Captain Edwards are kept in the Public Records office in London.
Access number ADM 2/120 S BP 491.

Original copies of the Admiralty's Enquiry into the loss of HMS *Pandora* are also in the Public Record Office in London.
Access number ADM 1/5330/2.

The manuscripts of the various journals kept by several of the *Pandora*'s crew and prisoners have been published. Captain Edward's and Surgeon Hamilton's journals were published in 1915 in:

Basil Thomson (Ed.) — *Voyage of HMS 'Pandora'; Despatched to arrest the mutineers of the 'Bounty' in the South Sea; being the narratives of Captain Edward Edwards R.N. (the Commander) and George Hamilton (the Surgeon).*
(Francis Edwards, London, 1915.)

Mutineer Peter Heywood's recollections were published in a biography in 1825:

John Marshall — *Royal Navy Biography or, Memoirs of the Services of all Flag Officers, Retired Captains, Post Captains and Commanders . . .*
(London, 1825.)

Mutineer James Morrison's journal was published in 1935 in:

Owen Rutter — *The Journal of James Morrison, Boatswain's Mate of the 'Bounty', describing the Mutiny and subsequent misfortunes of the Mutineers, together with an account of the Island of Tahiti.*
(Golden Cockerel Press, 1935.)

Midshipman David Renouard's account of the voyage in the *Pandora*'s tender was published in 1964 in:

H.E. Maude (Ed.) — The Voyage of the *Pandora*'s tender.
(*Mariner's Mirror* **50** (3): 217—35, 1964.)

A microfilm copy of Renouard's manuscript is held at the Mitchell Library in Sydney.
Access number MF CY Reel 515.

George Hamilton — *A Voyage Round the World in His Majesty's Frigate 'Pandora'.* Facsimile edition of the original 1793 Berwick edition. (Hordern House, Sydney, 1998).

Archaeological reports:

Graeme Henderson — Report to the Department of Home Affairs & Environment on the April 1979 Expedition to establish the identity and archaeological potential of the *Pandora* wreck.
(Unpublished report, Western Australian Museum, Fremantle, 1979.)

Graeme Henderson — *Pandora* Expedition 1983: Interim Report *et. al.*
(Unpublished report, Queensland Museum, Brisbane, 1984.)

Peter Gesner — The *Pandora* Project, reviewing genesis and rationale.
(*Bulletin of the Australian Institute for Maritime Archaeology*, Fremantle, 1988.)

Peter Gesner — HMS *Pandora*, situation report.
(*Bulletin of the Australian Institute for Maritime Archaeology*, Fremantle, 1990.)

J.N. Guthrie, L. Blackall, D. Moriarty & P. Gesner — Wrecks and Microbiology: a case study from the *Pandora*.
(*Bulletin of the Australian Institute for Maritime Archaeology* **18** (2): 19—24, 1994.)

Peter Gesner — HMS *Pandora*: 5 seasons of excavation.
(Cultural Heritage Series, *Memoirs of the Queensland Museum*, Brisbane, 2000.)

Janet Campell & Peter Gesner — HMS *Pandora*: an illustrated catalogue of artefacts.
(Cultural Heritage Series, *Memoirs of the Queensland Museum*, Brisbane, 2000.)

The *Bounty* Mutiny:

The most recent publications on William Bligh and the *Bounty* Mutiny are:

Gavin Kennedy —
Captain Bligh: the man and his mutinies.
(Duckworth, 1989.)

Greg Dening — *Mr Bligh's Bad Language: passion, power and theatre on the* Bounty.
(Cambridge University Press, 1992.)

William Bligh's own account of the *Bounty* mutiny was published in 1790 as:

William Bligh —
A Narrative of the Mutiny on Board His Majesty's ship Bounty. . .
(G. Nicol, London, 1790.)

(Available in a modern edition edited by Robert Bowman and published by Alan Sutton Publishing, Gloucester, 1981.)

A selection of documents relating to the *Bounty* mutiny have been gathered and edited by George Mackaness and published in:

George Mackaness (Ed.) —
The Book of the Bounty.
(Everyman's Library, London, 1981.)

Maritime Archaeology:

Keith Muckelroy —
Maritime Archaeology.
(Cambridge University Press, 1978.)

Graeme Henderson —
Maritime Archaeology in Australia.
(University of Western Australia Press, 1986.)

J. McKay, R Coleman —
The 24-gun Frigate Pandora 1779.
Anatomy of the Ship series
(Conway Maritime Press, London, 1992.)

J. Delgado (Ed.) —
British Museum Encyclopaedia of Underwater and Maritime Archaeology.
(British Museum Press, London, 1997.)

The Pandora Project:

www.Qmuseum.qld.gov.au
www.mtq.qld.gov.au

Special thanks

People from all over Australia and overseas have participated in and supported the five Queensland Museum *Pandora* expeditions between 1995 and 1999. The author gratefully acknowledges the assistance or support provided by his colleagues and peers at:

- Environment Australia (Heritage and Conservation Branch)
- Australian National Maritime Museum
- Royal Australian Navy
- Western Australian Maritime Museum
- Tasmanian Department of Primary Industries, Water and Environment
- Heritage Victoria
- South Australian Department of Environment and Heritage
- New South Wales Heritage Office
- Townsville General Hospital
- The Dive Bell
- James Cook University
- Museum of Tropical Queensland
- Queensland Museum
- The *Pandora* Foundation
- National Tidal Facility
- City of Townsville
- Townsville Port Authority
- Ergon Energy (NORQEB)
- Thuringowa Shire Council

And support from the following volunteers:
Peter Sullivan, Mark McCafferty, Len Zell, Kaye Walker, Colin Hodson, Heath Bell, Elizabeth Evans-Illidge, Paula Tomkins, Howard Smith, Nigel Erskine, Cos Coroneos, Annabel Wood, Mark Lawrence, Ian Lawrence, Vivienne Moran, John Read, Dennis Lee Sye, David Wood, Coleman Doyle, Stirling Smith, Brad Duncan, Jaco Boshoff, John Gribble, Rhiannon Walker, Jane White. Brian Richards, David Bell, Gavin Ericsson, Sean Rubidge, Kevin Hubbard, Graham Schulz, Greg Chapelow, Brian Dermody, Allison Mann.

The author, Peter Gesner, is head of the *Pandora* Project, and a Senior Curator of Maritime Archaeology at the Queensland Museum. Peter is based at the Museum of Tropical Queensland, Townsville. Since obtaining a postgraduate diploma in Maritime Archaeology from the Western Australian Institute of Technology in 1982, Peter has been professionally involved in Australian maritime archaeology and has worked on several shipwrecks in Western Australia and Victoria as well as in Queensland. Peter also has post graduate qualifications in Ancient History and Archaeology from the University of Amsterdam (The Netherlands).